How Not to Act

How Not to Act

TOP TIPS FOR ACTORS AND LIKE MINDED RANTS FOR AGENTS!!

By Pip

"An actors self-tape
is the only time they have
complete control of their
audition"

David James Coakley

PIP'S TIPS

HELLO

There will be people who ask, why am I writing this book...?

I can honestly answer, god knows why!!

I woke up one day and thought about all the questions I am asked by actors as an agent, and all the times I have repeated myself.

Then I was reminded of all the books I have bought and still not read and all the books I have been advised to read and I won't or don't have time...

Weekly my clients tell me about the workshops they have paid for or the courses they are doing and all I can think of is: how does everyone manage to pay for all this and is it not a tad repetitive?

Now. I am not an acting specialist and do not claim to be; I currently am not, nor have ever been an actor.

I managed people and businesses, and I am very good at making money in business. I am what you might call, the happy outsider looking into a world that is so cut throat, no wonder there is a lack of self-worth and personal growth at times...

But as crazy as it sounds I love it and I love my clients, I love the challenge of finding them auditions and I am emotionally invested in each and every one of them...

I am very much of the school, We are a team and without each other, we would, I mean I would, not be doing this job. Please remember: I am not teaching you to be an actor.

I am only advising you on your travels, giving you some insight on what frustrates agents and casting, some tips on marketing yourself as a business... With the intention "Like the stop smoking book" by Alan Carr, that by suggestive repetition you will start seeing your agent as a team member and not a pedestal to be revered at.

It's like that 'God complex' the agent has over their talent.

It's worth repeating the agent needs you as much as you need them in most cases...

So TEAM is moving forward...
If you take anything from this rant / book, I hope it is at least...

Be happy in what you do and believe in what you are doing .. because it's a lot easier for me to believe in you, if you believe in yourself...

Hugs

THOUGHTS FROM AN AGENT...

Agency Charges.

Rule number one and one of the most asked questions...

"Is it right an acting agent charges you to join their books...?"

"I have been offered a place in... And they are charging me for admin and website fees"...??

The answer GLOBALLY is...

NO

NB: Some children agencies do charge fees and I do believe this is OK... I don't work with children on the whole, and those I do, I have on the same contract with the parents - watch out though as some children's agencies charge you twice, one fee for modelling and one fee for acting, same web site !, they also tell you their chosen photographer... ?!

HEADSHOTS

Your Headshot should be you, no filters or fillers; They should be no more than a year old, as an adult actor.

Imagine going to an audition, you need to look like your Headshots. If You look 10 years younger or a few stones lighter/ bigger you will obviously not be going to get the part. You will also be wasting everyone's time. If you have an agent, they should nag you to keep your head shots updated.

This helps them and you to get work.

Headshots should be a selection of poses ..straight on, slightly to the side, left side to side right, and I would be inclined to ask for a full length photo as well because a lot of productions do ask for them nowadays.

Depending on what side of the world you're on, head shots are done slightly differently. I tend to prefer international exposure, which has more colour and slightly more personality. The days of dull background colours and neutral tops have come to an end, show your personality with a splash and stand out.

Smile! Don't look so serious.
I hate smiling, but I'm not an actor!

YOUR CV/ RESUME

The over complication of how to do a CV, it is a document once made that can be used and edited often, it does my head in, everyone has an opinion!...

Is there actually a right way? Is there a wrong way? Who knows, it depends on who you ask, what country you're in and if the wind is blowing in the right direction...

Personally, I think it's another way for someone to charge you on how to do it right, but there is no fixed right way...

But you need too...
Make it clear
Make it concise
Make it simple

In my humble opinion..!

Your name
Contact details.
Links to spotlight / actors' access, etc.
Photo at the top (left)
Work history. Newest at top Date, role, production company, location.
Training.
Skills.
Hobbies.

This makes it so simple for an agent, Casting Director or Production to see who you are and what you have done... Basically, I need to see within seconds, do you look the part, do you have the experience?

If I'm looking for a ballerina or elephant trainer, I'll be expecting a ballerina/ elephant trainer within the first jobs/ few jobs.

A note of caution here... Remember the skills are what you can actually do now... Not something you did as a child... Many times I have double checked a client's skill set before submitting them for a role... If you have not ridden a horse or jumped out of a building for years... Please take it from your skill set... Or take the hobby up again.

CV/ RESUME EXAMPLE

Bob, Bobby
Agent email or acting email
Phone number (if no agent)
Spotlight pin   23**-**89-9*9*9

Credits:
2024   Dog trainer on Mars - Love on Mars - Planet productions - Mars
2023   Ice cream maker Phil- Sahara desert living- sand productions - the desert
2010   Sgt Crappy name - The plastic Bill - BBC productions - Skegness

Training:
2000: BS Hons. Acting and performance in Classic art of talking rubbish..
1998: HND in toe nail painting

Skills:
Riding Elephants and house training Mice
Bar work and spilling coffee maker
Singing in the shower, Baritone, Tone deaf
Classic miming, eating fresh onions

Hobbies:
Reading, Swimming, Running backwards, Tripping over and flying through the air.

NB: this is a fictitious CV, all names and descriptions are made-up and should not be used in the real world!!

Own it ....

How many trained nurses, fire fighters pilots write in their title: "aspiring nurse", "pilot" or "fire fighter" ???

This is one of my pet niggles... how many actors do you see, writing "aspiring actor".... ?!

You are your brand and frankly this does not in still confidence in me ...

You're not wrong but then you're not right either!! ...

I believe strongly in manifestation.

Remember the three B's

Believe it , Be it , Become it ......

So if you're a elephant ballerina or horse poet... Own it!

WE HAVE CONTACT!

I get many emails requesting to be a part of the company and with every email I receive, I am honestly grateful but... and there are a few niggling points...!!!

1. Do your homework .. the people who write to me saying they are impressed with my awards or the programs my clients have been in , have shown me they   have no clue who we are .. and I will move on to the next email ...

2. I personally don't advertise any jobs and to be frank there are NO talent agency awards (that I am aware of!) Lot's of business awards though, so don't be fooled into thinking these awards make them good agents, they could be a good new business or a good boss, etc... So, investigate who you're writing too...

3. Don't do group and generic emails... Nothing worse than seeing every other agent you have written too, it basically shows that A) you are clutching at straws and B) you don't really care who reps you.

4. Don't waffle ... come to the point, and keep your links limited .. nothing worse than 15 different links!

5. Grammar and spell check... I am the worst at this and find I am as much to blame when I am writing... And just to be a complete hypocrite here, (because I can !) I will notice your grammar and spelling mistakes... So, take the time to check them.

Lastly.... know who you're talking to... my name is not BOB !!

AGENTS' DUE DILIGENCE

Do your research...

Every panel or actor I chat with about joining us or looking for an agent, I advise they check out the social media and ask other actors who are part of that agency for their thoughts and recommendations...

Depending on the country that you are in, there might be a governing body who could share with you their agency rosters that you could also check.

BUT bear in mind: NOT all good agents are signed up to those listings...

The best way is to go through another actor, get their feedback...
Don't judge their social media accounts for self-tape posts or confirmed jobs.

Not all agents feel the need to do this type of marketing to prove their worth or how busy they are (I do sometimes wonder though , how do you get the time to be on social media if you're THAT busy?!

Word of mouth is very powerful ...

WORKSHOPS

"So, my name's Bob, I have been acting for a while, I have done a few day player roles and I am making ends meet at present doing walk on roles...

So I thought what better way to make some money, doing workshops for all actors, to help them with their auditions and how to get them their jobs on the big shows/films."

Stop for a minute and re-read what I have written...

Actors who have no training to coach and who have not even made it into the industry, giving young and new actors lessons and advice on how they can make it in the industry...

Am I going mad ??!! These people have not made it there themselves. A day player role in a soap or a part in a movie does not make them experts!!?

Maybe I am just being a tad pedantic?... But seriously it's like the blind leading the blind at times... No??

Or my gosh... If a person has only been in one film for a minute, it does not make them a specialist or a top actor...

So please, like anything, check out who is doing the workshop before parting with your hard earned cash.

You need to be seen, you need to network and be on the radar of whoever is doing the productions but you do not have to kill yourself or go bankrupt going to multiple workshops a week or month...

Be selective.
Find the team that you really want to be seen by, look at the shows they cast and strategically work out which ones you can and need to see. One or two a month is plenty.

To Be Frank...
How many times have you paid for a workshop and had the same feedback and been told they will keep you in mind if anything comes up...

Has anything ever come up, even though you have seen a particular person multiple times??

I have heard actors getting upset because they can't afford all the workshops and feel they are failing...

Because they aren't being seen... Believe me, stop stressing.

Yes, you must network, and hone your skills... But you will be remembered if you did well in an audition and follow up after and say thank you.

I know lots of actors who pay to do courses that have links to TV shows and in the years they have paid to be there, they have never had a request to be on the show, despite being told they are on their minds!! So choose wisely ..

Remember :
The product of being an actor and the promise of opening doors for you , is becoming a cash cow, so spend wisely when honing in on your art ..

SELF TAPES

Before I really get into this exciting subject... Can I please advise, beg.... On behalf of all casting directors and talent agents..

READ THE BLOODY EMAIL, THE HEADING, AND ATTACHMENTS..

Then come and ask questions.. NONE of us mind helping, if we know you have read through and still don't understand or if like some of my clients you need help, just ask...

But to get the email and within 1 minute phone and ask questions, clearly showing you have not read a word... Or do the self-tape and completely miss the questions for the ident or the actions...

Well I can tell you it's annoying to say the least... So please stop... Read through everything and then move forward with the tape...

Only if you clearly know what you have to do...

Someone once said to me "the self tape process is the Only thing in your control " (wise words!) So Remember, it's that one chance... Each time you need to put your best foot forward... And don't rush...

Self-tapes in the world of Auditioning are relatively new. Prior to Lock-down and the pandemic, in person auditions were the only way to be seen.

The world opened up with self-tapes, which in turn has given many more opportunities to actors who don't live near or in the Major production hubs, it has helped with the finances as well of course. Casting has realised the benefits of all these additional actors...

But like all things there is a downside. The competition has gotten a lot tougher: Not having the in-person direction, and very rarely do you get feedback... (Even the agent does not get feedback most of the time).

Now the world is relatively back to normal. (If you can say anything is normal!). I personally hope and do not think that self-taping will disappear altogether for the first rounds of auditions, but I am seeing Recalls Becoming more in person.

(This is where you are being directed and seeing the chemistry between other players on the field so to speak.)

In regards to self-taping.. There are NO set golden rules but there are a few guidelines to follow.

Background / surrounding.
By having your background full of décor, your potentially Oscar/ bafta nominated acting skills are being diluted with the viewer looking at the stuff around you / over your shoulder...

I once watched a self-tape and remember thinking I knew that place on the painting behind him and asked the actor where they bought the painting from! SO if I am looking as an agent and having a good nose around what do you think someone else will be doing..!! ?

(Oh and while I am on this point.. Iron your sheets, if this is your choice of background, they would look so much better uncreased and shows you have and iron !!!)

LIGHTING

Amazon has great lighting rings, but nothing really beats daylight, however, we all know that most self-tapes are done in the evening after work or other life commitments.

Lighting is essential if you don't want to look like a mass murderer or a living corpse. A ring light from Amazon does the trick, they are not expecting huge rigs of lights and cameras, but just something that shows the contours of your face...

NO LIGHTING

HALF LIGHTING

TOO MUCH!!

SOUND

There is nothing worse than watching a self-tape and hearing a baby screaming in the background or the kids shouting... I have even heard a car crash during a tape, and the woman shouting at her husband, I won't say what I heard, but very choice words were screamed...

I must say! Needless to say sound quality is important and most good phones are good enough, but if you want to invest in a small microphone that attaches to your shirt then, it's an investment worth getting, especially if you are a quiet talker!

CAMERA ANGLE

I hate looking up at people's noses and counting their nasal hair.

It is also not the most flattering angle of one's face and weight issues, if you think you have any...

The camera height should always be mid chest up... Casting sometimes ask for closer or they might ask for full length.

Either way it's wise to FOLLOW the instructions given to you in the Audition notes and if you're not sure ASK !

HEADS IN SHOT PICTURE

ALL taping should be in landscape... A portrait does not make you look thinner or taller!! And it leaves black lines on either side of the tape when watching...
Most annoying...

All self-tapes unless stated on the notes given by casting should have an ident/ slate if you're in another country bar the UK again, unless audition notes say otherwise, general rule of thumb is you say NAME - ROLE - AGENT...

Your profiles: turn left, turn left again, turn to back of head, turn left again, and turn left again facing the front (360), then your hands: start palms away and then palms facing you...

And thank you...

Have fun and show your personality a bit here... I have someone who says it every time. This is my left side, my best side, my right side and I am back...

I smile every time because you can see he is having fun...

Now this is where I might differ in my thoughts of self-tapes. Casting already has an idea what you look like, so I tend to advise, unless otherwise directed in the audition email:

TV-Film go straight into action/scenes with your ident at the end. Commercial, ident THEN action/scenes.

There is a reason behind this madness and that's... If I was casting ,watching hundreds of tapes.

I already know its Bob, as the tape has been labelled, so by going straight into the scene they see you act and then if they like what they see they will watch the ident and see some of your personality.

(If You are a casting assistant/ director reading this... Please let me know if I have messed this up for you!) The book's in print now... But you could blame Bob!!

A tip that might help the frozen rabbit syndrome (when you're as stiff as a board and can't relax for the self tape)... read the script and try and get a sense of the scene...

Then play music...

Choose the appropriate piece that matches the mood of the script.. Dance to it...

Humm to it...

Then go into your character... Your body will then move in time to the tempo naturally... (Haha, I have just had a mental I age of many actors looking at me like I am mad!!!
It works... Try it !!)

Lastly on the subject of self-tapes...

Stop leaving them till the last minute. Sometimes being an agent is like being a parent, we can see when something has been rushed and it does not look good for either of us. I have refused to send tapes in, when they have been left till the last minute to be done...

The agent and the actor are supposed to be a team and your work reflects on the company as well as you. Oh on Another thought...

If you say you are going to do the tape, your agent will have told the casting a tape will be forthcoming...

But then when you decide that you can't do it or you forgot or medical emergency for your pet elephant or aliens came to earth and time just flew by...

We, the agents, have to then tell casting marks this down... So if you are com-mitted to doing this job, then do it, stop making excuses...

Oh my gosh and there is another thought.!! Sorry,. they are popping in my head like a popcorn machine!!

There is nothing worse for an agent to hear, "I did not see my emails". It becomes a tad tedious and time consuming chasing an actor down to see if they have seen the email or not... That time could be better spent looking for opportunities for you the actor. So with this in mind... Keep your email alerts on...

You chose to be in this mad world of the arts and you chose to have someone work hard for you, to find work... So why would anyone, then, not do the tapes (unless ill of course) or check their emails... It's madness!!

TEAM WORK

Look at the words above and there is No I in teamwork ...

There is nothing more disheartening as an agent, who does everything they can to get their clients work, to see actors do 'anonymous' posts slighting their agents ..

The golden rule is supposed to be, that you are a TEAM, this is why you need to have a relationship with that agent .. if you are not talking to your agent or they are not answering your emails then I agree you have a problem .. it's a two way street, the agent does have other clients , you need to be proactive as well and if the agent does not like it then again it's the wrong agent.

I agree there are some less desirable agents out there, but keep that open communication, whether they find work or you find work there should not be a divide...

Did you know the UK is about the only country in this industry with such a divide between actors and agents? Other countries see their agents as members of their teams and some have managers as well , but at no time are any members of the team excluded on a contract ..

One day I will ask that "anonymous" person,"... so would you work for free?"... Because if you keep getting cheaper paid jobs and are always unavailable for work.. Why would the agent then keep you on? Agents do have bills to pay as well .

So going back to the title of this chapter TEAM... it takes both parties to get where you want: the agent sits there looking for submissions all day every day and you also look on other sites ..together the more jobs you're suited to and submitted for the more you are seen and potentially chosen to audition ..

There is another actor agency relationship I have not got my head around yet either and that's Agency hopping... Yes it's a thing in the world , in the UK... Actors will sometimes only give an agency 3 months tops to show their worth before they go hunting for another agent.

It takes a few months to be seen and heard and then it's also down to what the industry is requiring ... . this all stems from the lack of TEAM being in their mind set...

It again, on a personal level is upsetting, because for you , I do all I can as an agent, invest in my clients, and in some cases they have multiple auditions and sometimes get the gigs and then they are poached by another agent within a year and it's like yep bye...

I guess that's the name of this game, but my gosh if an agent just got rid of actors like that, the actors would be in an uproar

I ask you is this Team work , jumping ship because someone is offering you the world ....? Please bear in mind most agents all work on the same platform and get the same breakdowns, so jumping ship does not always make sense.

MARKETING / BRANDING

Here I see your eyes rolling and questioning why this is relevant... Sadly this is one of the most overlooked parts of being an actor, you're trained to act, on screen/ off screen, on stage and in various other places, but no one is really looking into the notion that YOU the actor is a business and therefore you need to advertise yourself; otherwise, why/ how would any one know you're there...

It's kinda like a movie... It's been made, people have worked hard on it and now you want the public to come and watch it... How do you do that? You advertise, you talk/ shout about it...

So why are you, as the actor, not treating yourself as a business...
This is the least discussed or thought-out process in an actor's world. There is even a lack of awareness in the education courses on how to be a business - in some places you are taught to do a web site and even open a fictitious theatre...

This is a worldwide issue in all the arts, not just acting. The general rule of thumb is network, have a website and a CV and off you go... Frankly that's not going to get you far...

There are many books that you can read up on and if you have not fallen asleep you might be lucky enough to glean some hope - understanding of the steps forward to marketing and branding yourself.

Let me save you some money and give you some tips of what I have learnt and worked on in the past. (To a certain degree that is... Because I can preach, but it does not mean I follow my own advice...
If I had time and the inclination to work on these steps every day my following would be huge and I would be seen and recognised by a lot more people as it is. My days are spent looking for opportunities for my clients ! Oh and shouting for my dogs!!!)

First though let me break up two major misunderstandings here...

Marketing... This is your social media, your podcasts, this is showing people what you're doing, who you are etc ..your business cards. The marketing for the company are my fliers, my business cards, and my posts on social media.

Branding is you... It's the logo... So, for instance, APTM brand is the purple face that is put on everything I do (Website, business cards again, head shots).

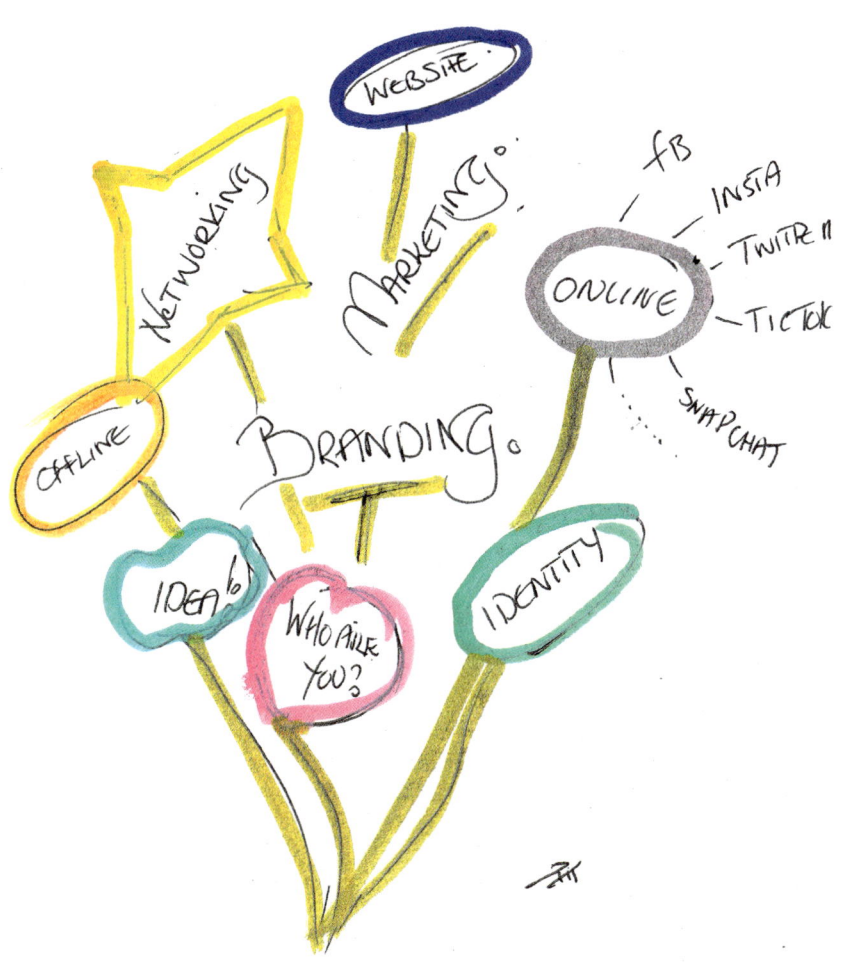

Basic Marketing 101...

Follow the people in the industry...

Casting directors, production houses...

Production teams first AD's, directors, producers... TV shows... Famous actors you respect... (Following people helps your algorithms).

Post regularly...

Not just about acting but about you...

Show people that you do have a life away from acting...

If you have two accounts, one professional and one personal, it is great to keep all those family things separate; however, your professional page should have a mixture of posts about you and your craft, and you as a person.

Follow Promoters

Post Regularly

Follow Casting

Engage in Posts

Social Media 101

IN PERSON AUDITION

PLEASE DON'T WALK INTO AN AUDITION WITH AN ATTITUDE... YOU ARE ALL ON THE SAME PAGE... NO ONE IS BETTER AND NO ONE IS WORSE.

Agent or not... YOU can only do your best ..
Listen to directions...

This is the job part of the work of acting... The actual gig is the fun part... So to speak.

LEGAL SIDE OF BEING AN ACTOR

I am asked on occasion about taxes etc as a working actor.

I am far from being a specialist on tax and employment...

The main thing that I know as an actor, is that you are considered self employed and should therefore register this part with your country's government site.

In the UK you will then get a code and this is what you will use every year for your self assessment forms .

Things do get slightly more complicated when you are also employed, so the best advice I can give on this subject is to speak to an accountant.

HOW TO LEAVE YOUR AGENT

Crazy I know, why would you want to leave your agent... Especially if it's me!!!

There are a number of reasons that come to mind and also that I hear when I interview new candidates.

Typically people move on when there is NO communication or they have had no jobs from the agent in the time they have been with them.

As a general rule though or should I say understanding, from an agent's perspective 3 months is definitely not enough time and 6 months... Seriously? Give an agent at least a year... Speak to them regularly and ask for break down lists.

Now before you go rushing into leaving your agent, make sure you have seen what they have submitted you for; ask them why you have not been getting auditions, and what can YOU do to help... Then if this does not work...

Have the decency to write and email and say , sadly you wish to move on...

A TEXT MESSAGE is not acceptable.

Just remember that the agent and you are a team... You work together, so it's only respectful that you part ways in a professional manner... (Plus it's a small world and some agents do talk to each other!).

(Now of course there are agents that do some things wrong and some agents who have been called out for dishonest behaviour... So the above does not apply and swiftly tell them to get lost, it's better to self represent than be around a CAD...

Please do remember though that NOT all agents are the same and some agents work very hard for their clients/ their team).

GHOSTING

I was once, on social media, called out for "Ghosting." The term means loosely ignoring someone! I admitted that I did not get back to this person and apologised, but, having the upper hand in the conversation, the person played the victim even more... Which did not fare well in the eyes of the onlookers...

But here are a few facts in my mad world...

If you have over 100 emails a day and on various platforms, you get messages from people, some you have reached out to and some you haven't, do you expect even the moist sanest of people to keep on top of all messages lets also add into the pot, the post cancer and preimenopausal brain, The submissions and the emails take precedence...

Like 99% of the world I am far from being perfect so I do forget...

There is always a phone number you can call... Maybe it's worth calling sometimes?

Just a thought!

AN AGENT'S RANT...
THE BITCHIN POSTS

Stop please thinking it's the agent's fault if you're not getting work... It's the agent's job to open the doors, it's the actors job to get the gig... And there can be loads of reasons why a person did not get a job... Do your audition and look forward to the next one...!

I repeat: You and your agent should be a team. Get a monthly breakdown on submissions, ask them what needs changing or doing. YOU also need to be proactive... Email casting occasionally, do submissions and talk with your agent...

The amount of actors I hear , who want to leave their agent as they haven't got any work but have had loads of submissions and some auditions and who have not been able to talk to their agent (or both), is overwhelming!

This is where I reiterate...
You are part of a team and if your agent is not having an open dialogue, make one or leave...

But leave for the right reasons, not because you have not got work...

(I had a person with me who had over 1.5k submissions in a year... In that they did 67 auditions and had numerous recalls and pencils, but not one job ... they left me and started with a new agent, this brief came out and I was like...

Will get that job it was so on point... And guess what they did... Casting even called me laughing saying about time, you guys have worked so hard...

It killed me to say, I wish... Was poached and joined another agent last week...) So going back to the beginning, because you do not get work, does not mean in most cases the agent is not working hard for you.

Oh while I am in a rant mode... Stop asking agents what jobs have they got their clients, when you are interviewing them... Ask them what auditions are you getting your clients...

IT IS NOT THE AGENT'S JOB TO WIN THE JOBS... IT'S THEIR JOB TO OPEN THE DOORS.

Nudges on spotlight:
Today I found out I am not the only agent that gets really frustrated by our clients who nudge us and clearly have not read all the brief...

The amount of times I have taken the extra time to go in and check the nudges to find its completely not suitable for that client...

Read the whole brief because you are wasting valuable submission time... And it's sooooooooooo annoying to be honest. (I can now see why some agents take that function away sadly)

SOCIAL MEDIA ACTOR RANTS ABOUT THEIR AGENTS

The 'anonymous' posts on social media about how bad an agent is not fair -

Are you one of them!!?...

I love to read some of the comments when I hear an actor say they have had so many auditions in a certain amount of time and that they have not got any of the jobs, and that they are thinking of leaving their agent as they have not found them work...

I mean seriously...

Let's put the shoe on the other foot... The agent has managed in a certain amount of time to get you many auditions...
You have done each and every one of these to the best of your ability...

But you have not got any of the jobs...

Should the agent now blame you and imply you are no good and therefore get rid of you for someone else??

Now, is it really OK for an actor to moan about an agent who is supposed to be their team member in this way and especially anonymously? Do you hear agents moan about actors the same way?

Also, it might be worth bearing in mind... Agents work on commission, they work 98% of the time for FREE for you, they want you to work as much as you do ..

MINDSET - MENTAL HEALTH

Back to nature... No I am not thinking or even suggesting running around in your birthday suit reconnecting with yourself and nature!!

I am thinking more along the lines of trying to ground yourself daily.

If possible, stand outside on a spot of grass, barefoot, face towards the sun and just feel the ground and the air around you...

This is something we as humans have stopped doing...

Feeling a part of this great universe... Since man became so busy and materialistic we have forgotten nature in its essence and what it can do for us...

CELEBRATE

I am a great believer in celebrating the wins. The audition is a win...
Meeting new people and networking is a win...

Stop second-guessing yourself... 2024 has been especially hard for some, with the knock on after effects of the union strikes in the States and not forgetting Covid...

Productions are down and more and more people seem to be coming into acting.

In fact, let's be fair. It's never really easy for any actor unless you're one of the 2%. Regardless of the year, doubting yourself is an ongoing battle that some actors face, especially when auditioning.

Can I do it?
Am I good enough?
What am I doing !!?

Can I, at this stage… give you some key pointers?…. (As if I haven't been rather opinionated the whole time!!)

ONE - you would not have been put forward for said audition if your agent (if you have one) did not think you were good enough.

TWO - YOU ARE GOOD ENOUGH >>> if you can not believe in yourself who can..?

THREE- The audition is the hardest part of the job… at this stage, you are potentially (vying) against hundreds if not thousands of other actors for the role. At this stage of the process, you are already ahead of them because you have the audition.

FOUR - YOU CAN DO THIS… YOU ARE GOOD ENOUGH!!

FIVE - Give yourself a break… you have trained for this, dreamed about this and hoped for this… So get up, shake yourself off, read over the directions… Take a breath and ENJOY…

(There is no point doing this job if it stresses you out). Be nervous by all means… But calling your agent at silly hours to freak out…

Remember THEY WOULD NOT HAVE PUT YOU UP FOR THE ROLE IF THEY DID NOT BELIEVE >Thank you R for inspiring this page.

TOP TEN TIPS FROM ACTORS

Ha ha this will be fun.. Making lists!!... That was my initial thought on the page and then the list became endless and I had to condense it.. So needless to say the humour of doing it faded.. Anyhow.. The top ten tips from working actors... with a few added on just in case!!

1. Be happy in what you do... Smile.

2. Read the instructions for self tape auditions at least twice.

3. Check self tape instructions for labelling before sending into either agent or casting.

4. Do not over think the tapes... do 3-4 takes only... 20 is too much.

5. Smile... Nothing is that bad!!!

6. Be your authentic self when meeting casting and production, it's you they are interested in.

7. Be prepared, learn your script.

8. Train... Keep the cobwebs off and keep improving your techniques.

9. Do not give up... The lack of self tapes or work does not always mean you are not good enough...

10. Don't take feedback personally, take the approach that all opinions are valued (OK this one is hard, some feedback is like a knife and I want to punch them, !!! Peace and love, breath in breath out... It's all good for the betterment of my career... Yadyyadyya!!!!!!!

EXTRAS TIPS

11. Be polite to crew and staff... Reputation on set is important.

12. Leave the last audition at the door... Open the doors to allow new ones in.

13. No one is waiting for you to come along but you have to trick them into thinking they want you.

14. Smile.

15. Keep profiles updated... Headshots should definitely look like you when you walk into a room.

16. Enjoy what you do.

SHOPPING LIST

LIGHTING
BACK DROP
TRIPOD WITH PHONE MOUNT

BUY THIS BOOK, IF YOU HAVE BORROWED IT !!

FROM ACTOR TO ACTOR

(Terry Bamberger: BA English certified teacher in dramatic arts and Senior instructor)

1. TRAIN. Find a class, find some acting buddies, set aside time to practise some scene work, to try out some character choices, to show some monologues, to work on voice & movement, sing. But do it, weekly.

2. Social Media Part II: Do it. It can be daunting or uncomfortable, but it's another way to creatively showcase your skills/artistry and to network. Some of the best gigs this year have been through indy films found via social media networking!

3. Expand your skills base – Accents, sports, stage combat, and smuggles jobs can also be a great.

4. Source for skills (baristas, teachers, bartenders, chefs, architects, nurses …) Add these skills to your CV and film short clips of you performing these skills!.

5. Read scripts. Watch movies. Watch plays. SEE PERFORMANCES.

6. DO YOUR HOMEWORK! Before you launch into any performance, don't "wing it!" Read the script/scene through at least five times. Get familiar with your character's word choice actions in the script, and score your script for wants/objectives and figure out how the character will achieve them (or not, via tactics). Make those choices. Rehearse, know your lines, THEN video the self-tape, or go on to rehearsals! Never go off to do a half-a**ss job – this is your job.

7. BRING YOU to your characters. Know and use your instrument (your body, mind, imagination) honestly to bring authentic performances to light. The interesting thing about actor performances are in the imperfections and human-ness of them, so no need to strive for perfection or "perfect" line readings!

8. Keep an ACTORS' JOURNAL. Write in it daily for affirmations, frustrations, celebrations, character & story ideas, people-watching observations. It's one way to keep sane and your mind actively exploring the human condition.

9. LOVE WHAT YOU DO. You must, as it's truly a marathon like no other.

10. KNOW YOURSELF. Be honest and explore and understand yourself. YOU are your instrument in this profession and the better you know it (how you respond to things, opinions, others, wants, desires, etc), the better you can play the notes and highlight aspects of yourself to bring authentic performances to your character work!

11. HAVE OTHERS SEE YOUR WORK. Show supportive people in your life performances you're working on. Get feedback – ask for feedback from your support group in the form of clarifying questions ("Why did you sit down when you said, 'Don't follow me?'" Vs "Oh, that was great/didn't like it when you sat down.") So that you know what isn't clear to an audience.

12. We don't create in a vacuum, you NEED this "outside eye" on what you are creating. You are the instrument and must have the audience's perspective on how things read or come across.

CASTING DIRECTORS BUGBEARS

1. Manners: Take the time to write the name of the person you are writing to...

2. Lack of research on what we have done...

3. Not labelling self tapes correctly...

4. Not following instructions, clearly set out in the emails...

5. Not keeping to the self tape audition deadlines...

Last but not least...

I am just a person, an agent, a mother, someone who likes wine and loves the warm weather... I make mistakes. I am not perfect...

I am not an actor or an acting specialist I went through many things in life to get here, but the biggest lesson I learned is to LIVE LIFE.

If you take nothing else from this fun little book...
What I would like you to take with you is the belief...

YOU ARE GOOD ENOUGH

Now Go and ENJOY the job you have always wanted to do or have done for years...

To all you veteran actors, new actors, writers, producers, directors, production teams, castings and of course agents I say Thank you...

Because our industry would not be here without you...

And a huge thank you to Terry Bamberger and Paul Izilein for all your help and advice in pulling this rant together.

Thank You x

LIST OF CASTING PLATFORMS

SPOTLIGHT

BACKSTAGE

CASTING NETWORKS

ACTORS ACCESS

E TALENTA

FILMMAKERS EU

NYCASTINGS

CASTING FRONTIER

CASTING TALENT

CAST CALLER

STARNOW

MANDY

IMDB PRO

ALL CASTING

INSTAGRAM HAVE CASTING CALLS
FACEBOOK HAS CASTING GROUPS
X DO CASTING CALLS as well

Casting Platforms

NOTES

NOTES

NOTES

NOTES

Printed in Great Britain
by Amazon

49308937R00048